Sacred Journey
Daily Reflections for Lent

To set out on any kind of journey, some degree of comfort and security is sacrificed for the sake of being able to move about more freely. Pilgrimages can begin with apprehension or enthusiasm, and much of being on a pilgrimage involves letting go of what is unnecessary so you can come to see what is truly necessary.

There is a 12-kilometre stretch of beach on the eastern shore of New Brunswick where I have walked many times, watching my children grow, skipping stones, and allowing thoughts to sort and sift. With each visit this long walk took on greater significance, as memories and possibilities for the future mingled with hopes and fears.

Those visits ended unexpectedly with the sudden ending of my marriage. I do not know if I will walk that beach again, but if I do, it will be a pilgrimage that brings to mind what every part of life's journey has taught me: that God is at the beginning and at the end of every path, and that hope is never far away.

Shane Parker
Answering the Big Questions

Wednesday February 6

Ash Wednesday

Joel 2: 12-18

Psalm 51: 1-4, 10-12, 15

2 Corinthians 5: 20 – 6: 2

Matthew 6: 1-6, 16-18

Jesus said to the disciples, "Beware of practising your piety before others in order to be seen by them…. Whenever you pray, go into your room and shut the door and pray to your Father who is in secret; and your Father who sees in secret will reward you."

Matthew 6: 1, 6

Henri [Nouwen] wanted everyone to spend a small amount of "quality time" each day in intimate prayer with the God of peace – being with God, experiencing God's peace, in order to be sent forth as instruments of God's love and peace. He taught that if we root our daily lives in the contemplative experience of being loved by God, we will help spread love around us and even be able to embrace and love our enemies.

"Only those who deeply know that they are loved and rejoice in that love can be true peacemakers," Henri wrote. "Prayer is the basis of all peacemaking precisely because in prayer we come to the realization that we do not belong to the world in which conflicts and wars take place, but to the One who offers us his peace." As he added, "By allowing ourselves quiet time with God we act on our faith that the peace we want to bring is not the work of our hands or the products of the movements we join, but the gift of Christ."

John Dear
Remembering Henri:
The Life and Legacy of Henri Nouwen

Thursday
February 7

Week After Ash Wednesday

Deuteronomy 30: 15-20

Psalm 1: 1-6

Luke 9: 22-25

Jesus said, "If any want to become my followers, let them deny themselves and take up their cross daily and follow me. For those who want to save their life will lose it, and those who lose their life for my sake will save it."

Luke 9: 23-24

When we discover and welcome God's call,
something beautiful happens in us:
we experience the love of God for us
and a whole new world opens up inside us.
We also realize that it is a very demanding call.
We are invited to leave our former,
familiar world,
and let go of what we used to know and hold on to;
 all this implies loss.
We receive something new
but at the same time we must let go
of something else….

Grief and loss are inseparable from the call.
If we accept the call but not the loss
we will live in contradiction.
When people make a decision,
for example to live in l'Arche,
but do not fully accept the consequences
of their decision,
it is a cause of great distress.
They constantly feel sorry for themselves,
sorry that they do not have a higher salary,

or more time for themselves,
shorter working hours, etc.
There is the call
and there is the loss.
But who wants loss?
When I left the navy more
than fifty years ago,
I sold everything I had,
which wasn't much,
and gave it to the poor.
Today I do not have much to sell
and I doubt if anyone would want
what I have!
But the call and the loss continue.
Today I am called to let go
of other things:
> attitudes, fears, prejudices, security, certitudes,
> the need to be in control…
There is a daily "letting go"
because each day Jesus is calling me
to become more loving, more compassionate,
more present to people,
more fully a child of God, more free from fear.

Jean Vanier
Befriending the Stranger

FRIDAY
FEBRUARY 8

WEEK AFTER ASH WEDNESDAY

Isaiah 58: 1-9

Psalm 51: 1-4, 16-17

Matthew 9: 14-15

Have mercy on me, O God,
according to your steadfast love;
according to your abundant mercy,
blot out my transgressions.

Psalm 51: 1

As the years pass and I become more comfortable with myself, less bothered by my imperfections and less frightened by my sins, I see that Christ's mercy is much more than his pity for our weakness or his willingness to forgive our sins. Christ's mercy is his never-failing presence in us and with us, whether we know it or not, whether we deserve it or not, and even whether we ask for it or not.

Christ's mercy is the presence of someone who is filled with compassion and total acceptance of us as we are; who does not condemn or reject us when we sin; who does not abandon us when doubts assail us and we think we are lost; who does not forget us when we are afraid or in pain but stays and suffers with us through it all.

To ask for mercy is to ask for love. It is to approach someone we love and trust totally, someone who loves us and knows us as we cannot ever love or know ourselves, who sees all our unreality and sin, and yet does not turn away from us even for a moment – someone who is always there.

Irma Zaleski
Finding Christ Within

Saturday
February 9

Week After Ash Wednesday

Isaiah 58: 9-14

Psalm 86: 1-6

Luke 5: 27-32

Jesus saw a tax collector named Levi, sitting at the tax booth; and he said, "Follow me." And he got up, left everything, and followed him.
Luke 5: 27-28

Thank you, God, for our past:
and all those who have beckoned us
towards your life.

Thank you for our present:
with its small callings, its stirrings in our souls,
its flashes of truth and its soundings towards love.
Make clearer your voice in the midst
of the clamourings,
conceive in us a fresh growing of love
and nourish it within our being
so that it comes forth in freedom.
Live in risen life in our midst, O God.

Thank you for our future:
before we know it, before we see it,
before we enter it,
in faith, we invite you to beckon us on, O God....
We commit ourselves to you
and our brave conversations together.
We will risk hearing each other,
trust ourselves to each other in faith
and await the presence of your Spirit among us.

Dorothy McRae-McMahon
Celebrations Along the Way:
Liturgies for Everyday Moments

SUNDAY
FEBRUARY 10

FIRST SUNDAY
OF LENT

Genesis 2: 7-9,
16-18, 25; 3: 1-7

Psalm 51: 1-4,
10-12, 15

Romans 5: 12-19

Matthew 4: 1-11

After being baptized, Jesus was led up by the Spirit into the wilderness to be tempted by the devil. He fasted forty days and forty nights, and afterwards he was famished.

Matthew 4: 1-2

There is a story of an acrobat in a small circus whose single act was to walk a tightrope without a safety net. Above the middle of the high wire was suspended a ring made of rope, soaked in gasoline and set alight. At times he would climb the ladder to the roll of the drums and start his walk, only to turn back. The crowds would jeer. At other times he would leap through the flaming circle. He said he was always scared, and the times he turned back were when his fear got the better of him. But when asked why he would attempt it in the first place, his answer was simple. He would say, "I know my life is on the other side."

When we follow our call we give up our security because our life is on the other side, in the living out of that call. But how do we know we are called? In fact, we are called by many things, so the question is knowing what is the right call. A true call engages us fully, carries us beyond ourselves, connects us, on a whole range of levels, with a reality that is both inviting and mysterious, compassionate and uncompromising. It is profoundly personal. It brings out the best in us and gives us a new and

→

more realistic understanding of ourselves. But in answering a call we also face our demons, as Christ did in the desert: we learn our limitations. We start to appreciate what is given to us on our path and to be grateful for that path and for the companions and adventures we have along that way.

So how can we distinguish a true call? By the fidelity of the one who calls us. That one is true to our relationship in good times and in bad; does not judge us as anything less than lovable and capable of loving; respects our individuality; celebrates with us what is good in life; works along with us in transforming what is damaging in our world; gives us the strength and the courage to hold what is suffering or damaged; lets us experience our freedom to be creative. The one who calls us truly shares with us all that he has and is.

John Pungente SJ *and* Monty Williams SJ
Finding God in the Dark:
Taking the Spiritual Exercises of St. Ignatius to the Movies

Monday
February 11

First Week of Lent

Leviticus 19: 1-2, 11-18

Psalm 19: 7-9, 14

Matthew 25: 31-46

"The righteous will [say], 'Lord, when was it that we saw you sick or in prison and visited you?' And the king will answer them, 'Truly I tell you, just as you did it to one of the least of these brothers and sisters of mine, you did it to me.'"

Matthew 25: 39-40

The word 'love' suffers, perhaps, from too good a press. It comes all gift-wrapped in pink ribbons and red hearts, and if we are not careful we will miss the point of it entirely. The most helpful thing I ever heard about love was this:

Love is not an emotion. Love is a decision.

If we honestly want to know what love means, we really do need to strip it of its emotional baggage, down to its bones and its marrow. If it has any bones at all, they will be about the *decision* to relate to another in a loving, life-giving way, and not the *feelings* that may or may not accompany that decision.

I once went to Lourdes, the famous shrine in southern France. Actually, if I am honest, I tried to *avoid* Lourdes, while travelling back north from the Pyrenees, but the autoroute had other ideas, and in spite of myself, I was suddenly there. I had wanted to avoid it because I expected it to be commercialized and full of religious kitsch, and it was.

→

But it also had love flowing through it like a river. I saw it in the eyes of the hundreds of people who had taken sick friends and relatives there, in hope that the journey might help them.

In countless faces I saw living evidence of the 'decision to love.' People who had given up their own chance of a holiday to tend the sick. Youngsters pushing the elderly and infirm in wheelchairs. Parents bringing up severely damaged children. I saw patience, and long-suffering, compassion, generosity, sacrifice, hope, trust ... love! It seemed to me that the miracle of Lourdes lay less in the occasional stories of those who would return home physically cured, and more in the continuous stream of indomitable human loving that flowed through its streets and its holy places.

These were individual people who were making a decision for love – a decision to do the more human, the more loving, the more life-giving thing in the circumstances in which they found themselves. You don't need to go to Lourdes to see this kind of 'elected love.' You can see it wherever individuals are dedicated to putting the needs of others before their own immediate wishes.

Margaret Silf
Roots and Wings:
The Human Journey from a Speck of Stardust to a Spark of God

Tuesday February 12

First Week of Lent

Isaiah 55: 10-11

Psalm 34: 3-6, 15-18

Matthew 6: 7-15

"Pray then in this way: 'Our Father in heaven, hallowed be your name. Your kingdom come. Your will be done, on earth as it is in heaven.'"

Matthew 6: 9-10

At the heart of Christian prayer is the prayer of Jesus, known as the Lord's Prayer. An integral part of this prayer is a recognition of the primacy of God's will. Praying oneself into the will of God becomes even more significant as Christians reflect on Jesus kneeling under the ancient olive trees in the early hours of Good Friday in the Garden of Gethsemane, overlooking the dark Kidron Valley and the walls of Jerusalem above it. Jesus falls on his face and prays, "My Father, if it is possible, let this cup pass from me; yet not what I want but what you want."

It may well be that the only worthwhile prayer is that which draws us into a closer understanding of the movement and development of God's will. To pray in this way is to place your own particular concerns in the context of a much more intricate and expansive whole, where who you are and what you seek can only be fully grasped when the wider sweep of God's hand is felt.

Shane Parker
Answering the Big Questions

WEDNESDAY
FEBRUARY 13

FIRST WEEK
OF LENT

Jonah 3: 1-10

Psalm 51: 1-2, 10-11, 16-17

Luke 11: 29-32

Create in me a clean heart, O God, and put a new and steadfast spirit within me....

The sacrifice acceptable to God is a broken spirit; a broken and contrite heart, O God, you will not despise.

Psalm 51: 10, 17

The important things in life, one way or another, all leave us marked and scarred. We never stop remembering our triumphs. We never stop regretting our losses. Some of them mark us with bitterness. But all of them can, if we will allow them, mark us with wisdom. They transform us from our small, puny, self-centred selves into people of compassion. For the first time, we understand the fearful and the sinful and the exhausted. They have become us and we have become them as well. We recognize the down-and-out in the street who mirrors our despair. We commiserate with the anger of the marginalized. We identify with the invisibility of the outcast. We can finally hear the rage of the forgotten.

Then and only then can the world really have hope that we ourselves are worth having hope in. Then and only then can we take back our power, break the barrier of isolation, transcend our limitations, find the hope in ourselves that emerges out of struggle, that refuses to give in to despair, that lives only in us.

Joan D. Chittister
Scarred by Struggle, Transformed by Hope

Thursday February 14

First Week of Lent

Esther 14: 1-5, 12-14

Psalm 138: 1-3, 7-8

Matthew 7: 7-12

> *"Ask, and it will be given you; search, and you will find… In everything do to others as you would have them do to you; for this is the law and the prophets."*
>
> *Matthew 7: 7, 12*

We were camping in a little place near Magdala, and it happened to be the Day of Atonement (Yom Kippur), during which, we learned, nothing might be bought or sold, and no one must be in transit on the roads, either on foot or by any other mode of transport. To our horror we discovered that the sales prohibition also included water, and that we were going to have to stay in our little tent all day without any. As the morning advanced, our tent turned into a tandoori oven and I was feeling really groggy. In desperation we set off to find some water, and persuaded a local Palestinian to let us have some. Like Jesus before him, this man broke the rules to help us in our need and we broke the rules ourselves, by walking the roads on the holy day. We broke the rules because the call of life was more insistent.

I remember with thankfulness the good man who gave me fresh water that day, and I remember how Jesus repeatedly stressed that the calls of love take priority over the strict demands of the law.

Margaret Silf
Roots and Wings: The Human Journey from a Speck of Stardust to a Spark of God

FRIDAY
FEBRUARY 15

FIRST WEEK OF LENT

Ezekiel 18: 21-28

Psalm 130: 1-6

Matthew 5: 20-26

"When you are offering your gift at the altar, if you remember that your brother or sister has something against you, leave your gift there before the altar and go; first be reconciled to your brother or sister, and then come and offer your gift."

Matthew 5: 23-24

Reconciliation is mutual forgiveness: an interpersonal process in which the persons involved experience the mutuality, trust, safety, compassion and nonviolence they need to be able to ask for and receive forgiveness from each other. There is a mutual desire to renew and rebuild the relationship. This is an interdependent and interconnected movement away from resentment, revenge and retaliation to mutual healing of hurts and a re-establishment of trust.

Reconciliation is the apex of communion and the epitome of community. In forgiving and being forgiven, we are reconnected in community. Community is a process and a journey that requires openness, listening-dialogue, respect, equality and reciprocity.

Janet Malone
Transforming Conflict and Anger into Peace and Nonviolence: A Spiritual Direction

Saturday February 16

First Week of Lent

Deuteronomy 26: 16-19

Psalm 119: 1-8

Matthew 5: 43-48

"You have heard that it was said, 'You shall love your neighbour and hate your enemy.' But I say to you, Love your enemies and pray for those who persecute you."

Matthew 5: 43-44

To forgive our enemies does not mean condoning or forgetting the evil they have done; it does not mean not trying to prevent them from committing it, or letting them go free to commit it again. In every human society, the innocent must be protected and the evildoer must be contained and prevented from doing more harm.

Nor does loving our enemies mean forcing ourselves to acquire any tender feelings towards those who have done us harm. It does not mean denying that they have done us wrong. It does not mean absolving them from the necessity of repenting for their crimes or from having to face the consequences of their acts. Even God will not do those things.

To love and forgive our enemies means refusing to allow the evil they have done to us to infect our own hearts and lives with its poison, and thus to spread it further in the world. It means refusing to hate them or to seek revenge on them, however hurt or angry we may feel. It also means being willing to give them another chance to repent and change, if it is reasonable to expect such a change and if it does not put the safety of others at risk.

In other words, to love and forgive our enemies means trying to put our hurts and anger aside – not denying that we have been hurt, but refusing to act out of our hurt. It means trying to see those who hate us as God sees them: mean and cruel, perhaps, needing to be stopped from doing further harm, and yet each a human being, one of those whom Christ has told us to love.

Irma Zaleski
Finding Christ Within

Sunday February 17

Second Sunday of Lent

Genesis 12: 1-4

Psalm 33: 4-5, 18-22

2 Timothy 1: 8-10

Matthew 17: 1-9

Jesus took with him Peter and James and his brother John and led them up a high mountain, by themselves. And he was transfigured before them, and his face shone like the sun, and his clothes became dazzling white.

Matthew 17: 1-2

Our time, our stories about ourselves, our histories are the best we can do from where we stand and look; but God's perspective can do strange things with history, and we are not the best judges of the meanings of our lives... [and] what shows God to the world. But we are given a glimpse of what God can do in this rare moment of direct vision, when the "door of perception" is opened by and in Jesus, and the end of the world is fleetingly there before us. And finally, we can let ourselves contemplate the fact that the divine freedom shown us in this vision tells us both that there is no escape from the world in which we have been put as creatures *and* that there is nowhere from which God can be finally exiled. This is the great challenge to faith: knowing that Christ is in the heart of darkness, we are called to go there with him…. If we have seen Jesus' glory on the mountain, we know at least, whatever our terrors, that death cannot decide the boundaries of God's life. With him the door is always open, and no one can shut it.

Rowan Williams
The Dwelling of the Light: Praying with Icons of Christ

MONDAY
FEBRUARY 18

SECOND WEEK OF LENT

Daniel 9: 3-10

Psalm 79: 8-13

Luke 6: 36-38

"Be merciful, just as your Father is merciful. Do not judge, and you will not be judged; do not condemn, and you will not be condemned."
Luke 6: 36-37

Living each hour as though it were her last transformed [Etty] Hillesum's hatred of the Germans to sorrow, a universal feeling for both the Jews and the Germans. In 1942, a year after she had begun her diary, she was able to say, "Do not relieve your feelings through hatred, do not seek to be avenged on all German mothers for they, too, sorrow at this very moment for their slain and murdered sons." Living with such sorrow gives it that sacred space essential for healing. Otherwise, hatred and revenge violate that inner space, wreaking more sorrow, hatred and revenge. "If you have given sorrow the space its gentle origins demand, then you may truly say, life is beautiful and rich."

Hillesum noted that hatred can be petty, with passing incidents being excuses for hatred. Indignation, on the other hand, must run deep and get to the core issues of injustice, violence and oppression. Hillesum's inner freedom and lack of fear continued as the Jewish atrocities increased. Although she still spoke about her fear, she continued to write and to hope, noting that "true peace will come when every individual finds peace within."

Janet Malone
Transforming Conflict and Anger into Peace and Nonviolence: A Spiritual Direction

TUESDAY FEBRUARY 19

SECOND WEEK OF LENT

Isaiah 1: 10, 16-20, 27-28, 31

Psalm 50: 8-9, 16-17, 21-23

Matthew 23: 1-12

Jesus said, "The scribes and the Pharisees sit in Moses' chair; therefore, do whatever they teach you and follow it; but do not do as they do, for they do not practise what they teach."

Matthew 23: 1-3

Letter to the Bishop

You ask why I disobey you, my bishop;
I answer in a spirit of prayer,
as I hope you did too in addressing me.
I, the Abbess, disobey, and all my sisters
choose to disobey,
because in such obedience is only darkness.
In our disobedience is light for our spirits,
so has God shown us.

I am not just disobedient,
I am outraged.
A thunderstorm of outrage shakes my soul.
In God's truth I say to you:
"You are wrong and we are right."

We are obeying Christ,
we are following Christ,
we choose not to insult Christ,
as obeying you would force us to do.

Because of what you call our disobedience,
you have forbidden us to sing our psalms.
You have deprived us of the Food of Life.
You have cut off the streams of life,
the sacramental graces.

The convent now is silent.
Our songs have ceased, as you asked.
We faint from lack of sustenance, as you command,
(we are not, after all, unreasonable);
but I can still speak to you for my sisters,
and this is what I have to report:

As we at first succumbed to sadness,
God spoke to us and said:
"This is not good.
How can you be forbidden to come to me – even by bishops?"
God, your Excellency, has told me to tell you this.

God said, "Listen to the psalms saying:
'Let everything that has breath praise God.'"
And you command us to be silent.

God said, "Tell the Bishop he is living by outward reality;
I want you to turn to inner reality."

So, for our part,
though still silent,
we have turned all our energies inward.
We have directed our inner selves towards God;
we sing in our hearts.
Our eyes greet one another and smile in song.
Our lips beam with God's silent praises, louder than any hymn.
There is not one outward sound,
but the house rings with the energy of our praise.

The angels seem to have come among us;
their sweet souvenirs of heaven can be heard in the halls.
The holy prophets of God walk the orchard paths with us,
the heavenly harpists have come to dwell in Bingen.

We do not touch the musical instruments with our hands,
but we breathe on them as we pass,
and what heavenly music we hear in our hearts.
We obey you where you are in outward reality
but in our hearts, we walk with God, and God with us.

God told me to tell you this also:
"Beware of closing the mouths of those who sing God's praises."
"Who dares to destring the harp of heaven?" God asked me.
"Only the devil," I whispered.

Ask yourself, O bishop, whose side are you on?

As for us, we sing in silence,
and we have discovered that
our soul is symphonic.

And I heard a voice saying:
"Who created heaven?" God.
"Who opens heaven to the faithful ones?" God.
"Who is like God?" Nobody.
So, O bishop, do not resist God,
lest you really discover the power of God.
With respect I write, and in God's name.

(Abbess Hildegard [of Bingen, age 80])

Mary T. Malone
Praying with the Women Mystics

Wednesday February 20

The mother of the sons of Zebedee came to Jesus with her sons, and kneeling before him, she asked a favour of him.... She said, "Declare that these two sons of mine will sit, one at your right hand and one at your left, in your kingdom."
Matthew 20: 20-21

Second Week of Lent

Jeremiah 18: 18-20

Psalm 31: 4-5, 13-15

Matthew 20: 17-28

The people with developmental disabilities have little sense of competition. They prefer to share with others rather than compete with them. It is interesting to watch them at l'Arche on the playing field. They enjoy being together just throwing or kicking a ball around without choosing teams and turning it into a competition. Even when occasionally they do choose teams for a game of soccer, no one bothers to keep score. The joy comes from playing and not from trying to defeat someone. My friend Doug McCarthy, a Jesuit from Canada, spent a summer at l'Arche in France. One afternoon he was helping people train for the Special Olympics. Claude was having a great time fooling around instead of trying to improve his running ability. Doug, losing patience, scolded him, saying, "Claude, if you don't smarten up, even Jean-Pierre is going to beat you." Jean-Pierre, being very spastic, could hardly walk, let alone run. Claude lit up with a great smile and said, "Wouldn't it be great if Jean-Pierre won!"

Bill Clarke SJ
Enough Room for Joy: The Early Days of l'Arche

Thursday February 21

Second Week of Lent

Jeremiah 17: 5-10

Psalm 1: 1-6

Luke 16: 19-31

> "There was a rich man who was dressed in purple and fine linen and who feasted sumptuously every day. And at his gate lay a poor man named Lazarus, covered with sores, who longed to satisfy his hunger with what fell from the rich man's table."
>
> *Luke 16: 19-21*

There is a story of a fearsome wolf that used to terrorize a village. At first the villagers ignored it, but after two or three fatal attacks, they became more and more defensive, but they couldn't decide how to deal with the problem of the wolf. Some of them said, 'We must go out there and kill the wolf.' Others said, 'We must build such a high fence around our village that nothing will ever be able to harm us.' Eventually they went to consult the Wise Man of the Woods who lived nearby. He listened to their story and then gave them his advice: 'Go home, and feed the wolf.'

The villagers were shocked and angered by this advice, and at first refused to act upon it. But gradually one or two brave souls started to put out food for the wolf, food that was eagerly taken. Soon the village had become used to the wolf, and the wolf had become almost tame. No longer driven by its raging hunger, it ceased to be a threat. But to get to the point of actually 'feeding the wolf,' the villagers had to ally themselves with fear's opposite

→

twin, 'trust.' They had to trust themselves and the wolf enough to make that first tentative contact. And they had to open their minds and their imaginations enough to understand the reasons for the wolf's attacks, and then try to address the underlying problem – the wolf's hunger.

Of course, life isn't as simple as this story might suggest. Even so, it is often true that when we befriend our fears, they turn out to be less fearsome than we thought. It has been wisely said that what we most acutely fear may actually be a blessing if we can face it and befriend it. It may be the greatest catalyst for growth that we have.

Margaret Silf
Roots and Wings:
The Human Journey from a Speck of Stardust to a Spark of God

**FRIDAY
FEBRUARY 22**

SECOND WEEK
OF LENT

1 Peter 5: 1-4

Psalm 23: 1-6

Matthew 16: 13-19

When Jesus came into the district of Caesarea Philippi, he asked his disciples, "Who do people say that the Son of Man is?"

Matthew 16: 13

"Who is Christ?" became a kind of koan for me – one of those apparently unanswerable questions that Zen Masters set for their students to solve. The students nearly always begin – as I had done – by trying to figure out the answer by puzzling and agonizing over it with their thinking minds. They sit on their mats "thinking, thinking, thinking," as a Korean Master once said to me, even though they have been told countless times that thinking will not take them there, that only "not-thinking" will.

The purpose of assigning a koan is to make the students experience "not-thinking" for themselves. If they persevere in their practice, the masters say, they will eventually, often only after many years, come to a stone wall of not-knowing that they cannot break through with their heads. Beyond the wall lies a mystery, a level of reality not accessible to rational thought.

At that moment, if the students do not panic but remain silent and still at the wall, they may discover that although the answer to a koan cannot be found by thinking, it can be found. It can come to them in a moment of insight that arises from the deepest layer of their being, their true mind. And when it comes it dispels, even if only for a few seconds, all the unreality and confusion that usually fill the human mind. It is this moment of insight that, in the Buddhist tradition, is called enlightenment. We become simply aware of who we really are and realize that there is nothing else we need to be.

I did not stay in Zen practice long enough to experience a moment of such enlightenment or to find the answer to the koan of Christ, yet I stayed long enough to realize how I must look for it. I could not find it by thinking about it or by studying and reading books. The true answer would not be a concept or a definition *about* Christ, but Christ himself: realization of his presence with me and in me, at the core of my being.

Irma Zaleski
Finding Christ Within

Saturday February 23

Second Week of Lent

Micah 7: 14-15, 18-20

Psalm 103: 1-4, 9-12

Luke 15: 1-3, 11-32

"So he set off and went to his father. But while he was still far off, his father saw him and was filled with compassion; he ran and put his arms around him and kissed him."

Luke 15: 20

Rembrandt, in his painting of the prodigal, has caught the gaze on the father's face, and then as we turn to look at those two hands placed on the son's shoulders, we see the one so firm and strong, the other so gentle. There is no escape from that loving gaze, even though I turn my back. In an extraordinary sermon, Austin Farrer speaks of those eyes and those hands, and how strong is a love which refuses to give up in spite of all resistance and every failure to respond:

> My back is turned to him,
> I have been told that he forgives me,
> but I will not turn
> and have the forgiveness,
> even though I feel the eyes on my back.
> But God does not give up:
> for he takes my head between his hands
> and turns my face to make me smile at him.
> He has taken a pair of human hands
> with which to turn our stiff-necked heads,
> and bring our eyebeams
> into line with his own.

Esther de Waal
Lost in Wonder

SUNDAY
FEBRUARY 24

THIRD SUNDAY
OF LENT

Exodus 17: 3-7

Psalm 95: 1-2, 6-9

Romans 5: 1-2, 5-8

John 4: 5-42

A Samaritan woman came to draw water, and Jesus said to her, "Give me a drink."

The Samaritan woman said, "How is it that you, a Jew, ask a drink of me, a woman of Samaria?" (Jews do not share things in common with Samaritans.) Jesus answered her, "If you knew the gift of God, and who it is that is saying to you, 'Give me a drink,' you would have asked him, and he would have given you living water."
John 4: 7-10

The Samaritan woman was an ordinary woman doing ordinary things who got an extraordinary insight into the fullness of life and was given an extraordinary task in a pagan world and they listened to her. She was a prophet, an unacceptable evangelist, a powerless figure, an apostle without portfolio. She wasn't a man – and she was to give the greatest testimony of all time. She wasn't a Jew – and she was to announce the Messiah. She was neither politician nor priest, and she was given the gift of understanding and living water and power and empowerment. And they listened to her.

Well, there's a revolution going on in today's church, too. Like the Samaritan woman, people, very ordinary people, are discovering the energy and the insight and the power that comes with the spiritual life. And as it happens when the Holy Spirit gets out of the chanceries of the world, quite ordinary people are being spiritually empowered to seize some gospel decisions of their own. They've come to some spiritual conclusions: that sexism is a sin, that peace is possible, that socialism is not all bad, that capitalism is not all good, that authority has limits and that the Word of God lives, too, in them.

And they're proclaiming those things. And they're demanding those things and they're living those things in the name of the gospel of Jesus Christ. Why? Because Jesus has turned their very ordinary selves, too, and their very ordinary lives into an extraordinary awareness of the presence of God – in them as well as in the powers that be. They have discovered the spirituality that empowers and, like the Samaritan woman, they will not be silenced.

Joan D. Chittister
In the Heart of the Temple

MONDAY FEBRUARY 25

THIRD WEEK OF LENT

2 Kings 5: 1-15

Psalm 42: 1-3; 43: 3-4

Luke 4: 24-30

Jesus came to Nazareth and spoke to the people in the synagogue: And he said, "Truly I tell you, no prophet is accepted in the prophet's hometown."

Luke 4: 24

To be empty and full at the same time – a paradox of our encounters with God, wherever they happen. Only as we empty ourselves and pour out to God our deepest longing do we find God filling our souls with living water that seeps into the well from which we draw our daily lives. Paradox beats at the heart of Jesus' identity, that very earthy life in whom the holiness of God takes flesh. George MacLeod points us to this paradox in his prayer: *"Invisible we see you, Christ above us, Christ beneath us, Christ beside us."* Only as we divest ourselves of what we expect Christ to look like are we given a glimpse of his surprising smile in eyes that meet ours – at our daily bus stop or in the exchange of his peace.

Nancy Cocks
Invisible We See You: Tracing Celtic Threads Through Christian Community

TUESDAY FEBRUARY 26

THIRD WEEK OF LENT

Daniel 3: 25, 34-43

Psalm 25: 4-9

Matthew 18: 21-35

Peter came and said to Jesus, "Lord, if a brother or sister sins against me, how often should I forgive? As many as seven times?" Jesus said to him, "Not seven times, but, I tell you, seventy-seven times."

Matthew 18: 21-22

Forgiveness means that we dare to face what we have done. We dare to remember all of our lives, with the failures and defeats, with our cruelties and lack of love. We dare to remember all the times that we have been mean and ungenerous, the ugliness of our deeds. We dare to remember not so as to feel awful, but so as to open our lives to this creative transformation. It does not leave us as we are, as if nothing we did ever mattered. If we step into that forgiveness, then it will change and transform us. Whatever is sterile and barren will bear fruit. All that is pointless will find meaning. At the end of *Lord of the Rings*, Sam scatters around the barren shire the magical fertilizer that the elves have given him, and the next spring every tree blossoms. That is an image of forgiveness.

Timothy Radcliffe
Seven Last Words

Wednesday February 27

Third Week of Lent

Deuteronomy 4: 1, 5-9

Psalm 147: 12-20

Matthew 5: 17-19

> *"Do not think that I have come to abolish the law or the prophets; I have come not to abolish but to fulfill. For truly I tell you, until heaven and earth pass away, not one letter, not one stroke of a letter will pass from the law until all is accomplished."*
>
> Matthew 5: 17-19

The hardest line taken by the Vatican was in dealing with divorced Catholics. The increasing numbers of divorced families lived a shadow existence in church communities. If they wanted their new marriages blessed, they would have to leave behind the faith that had nurtured them. Costello, the lone wolf, continued to welcome the divorced....

Dan Bagley says Costello's willingness to provide the sacraments to people whom the Church would otherwise reject was based on his belief that he was simply doing what Jesus would have done.

"Jesus always took people where they were at. If a marriage broke up, it broke up. Costello would say you have to treat people with dignity, make them feel good about themselves and welcome them back in so they can get on with their lives. If parents who weren't married came to have a child baptized, Costello would welcome them in. He believed that every child should be given the graces of the church."

Charlie Angus
Les Costello: Canada's Flying Father

**THURSDAY
FEBRUARY 28**

**THIRD WEEK
OF LENT**

Jeremiah 7: 23-28

Psalm 95: 1-2, 6-9

Luke 11: 14-23

O come, let us sing to the Lord; let us make a joyful noise to the rock of our salvation!

Let us come into his presence with thanksgiving.

Psalm 95: 1-2

"If there is any word that should characterize the life of peacemakers, it is 'gratitude,'" Henri [Nouwen] wrote. "True peacemakers are grateful people who constantly recognize and celebrate the peace of God within and among them." Henri taught that if we are going to spend our lives resisting war, poverty and nuclear weapons and not give in to despair because of apparent ineffectiveness, we need to count our blessings, to celebrate life, and to be grateful for simple gifts: being alive, being healthy, being loved by God and others, being called to love and serve others. Henri urged people to practise gratitude as a daily discipline to overcome the tendencies towards cynicism, bitterness, mean-spiritedness, resentment and violence. If we are grateful to God and others, peace will flourish within and around us. It will extend forth to lead those around us from pain, anger, despair and violence to know the peace of gratitude.

John Dear
*Remembering Henri:
The Life and Legacy of Henri Nouwen*

Friday February 29

Third Week of Lent

Hosea 14: 1-9

Psalm 81: 5-16

Mark 12: 28-34

Jesus answered, "'You shall love the Lord your God with all your heart, and with all your soul, and with all your mind, and with all your strength,' [and] 'You shall love your neighbour as yourself.'"

Mark 12: 30-31

Love of neighbour, but especially love of our enemies, is a difficult task in the spiritual life that hasn't changed since the days of Eckhart. The Meister shifts the focus for testing this love from an external consequence to the internal principle of such love, which is the capacity to truly love our self. In speaking of learning to love our truest self, Eckhart is not referring to egoism: he means our common human nature. This nature we share with all women and men, but especially with the God-Man Jesus Christ. The sail that catches only half the wind is a pastoral illustration, sensitive in its concession that most of us can't love this perfectly. Yet it stresses our capacity to learn to love our true self so as to love others. For some of us, this love might only extend to a friend. This is clearly a start; at least such a person is upon the Seas of Love.

Michael Demkovich OP
Introducing Meister Eckhart

Saturday March 1

Third Week of Lent

Hosea 5: 15 – 6: 6

Psalm 51: 1-2, 16-19

Luke 18: 9-14

"Two men went up to the temple to pray, one a Pharisee and the other a tax collector.... The tax collector, standing far off, would not even look up to heaven, but was beating his breast and saying, 'God, be merciful to me, a sinner!'"

Luke 18: 9, 13

The Pharisee is right: he is not like the tax collector, but not quite the way he imagines. He thinks he is better than such a sinful individual, but that very thought negates any spiritual benefit his otherwise positive actions could have brought him.

In contrast, by acknowledging his sinfulness the tax collector is forgiven. Since what matters in prayer is the attitude of the heart, Jesus announces that the tax collector is the one whose prayer was heard and who was justified by God. In the Bible, to be justified means to stand in a right relationship with God. In the First Testament this relationship was expressed in terms of the covenant that, by its very nature, links our relationship with God to our relationship with others. One irony of the parable is that the Pharisee, a member of a group that went out of its way to preserve the covenant with God, had actually broken it. By cutting himself off from those he thought beneath him, he also cut himself off from God.

John L. McLaughlin
Parables of Jesus

Sunday March 2

Fourth Sunday of Lent

1 Samuel 16: 1, 6-7, 10-13

Psalm 23: 1-6

Ephesians 5: 8-14

John 9: 1-41

As Jesus walked along, he saw a man blind from birth.... He spat on the ground and made mud with the saliva and spread the mud on the man's eyes, saying to him, "Go, wash in the pool of Siloam."

John 9: 1, 6-7

[Jesus] listened to my plea all right. I could *feel* him listening. It felt as though every particle of him was focused entirely and exclusively on *me*. That was such a good feeling. No one had ever done that before. It was almost worth being blind for. When I'd told him my tale, he kicked off by debunking the whole myth of it being either my parents' or my own fault. 'That's not how God is,' he thundered. '*When* will people understand?'

Then, turning his attention back to me, he asked me to tell him about myself – what I did all day, and how I felt about things. It didn't take long to tell him how I spend my days. I sit here, me and my begging bowl, and together we listen to the world go by, and especially we listen for the clink of a shekel in the bowl. Enough of those, and that means some dinner tonight. How do I feel about it? What kind of question was *that*? How did he imagine I would feel about it? I want to see again, of course.

'*Do* you? *Really*?' he interjected.

I was livid. This man was winding me up. What blind beggar wouldn't want to see again? What was that comment supposed to mean?

He must have been reading my thoughts. 'Tell me,' he spoke thoughtfully and slowly. 'Do you want to be healed? Think about what it means to be whole, to see again, to live a normal life. Think. And then tell me truthfully, do you want to be healed?'

I thought! I'd never done that before. I thought of all the things I could do if I had my sight. I could work. I could earn a living. I could participate in the community. I could even think about more intimate relationships ... I thought, as he told me to. And you know what – the thoughts appalled me!

Imagine, at my age, how would I learn a trade? How would I find a job in this ruthless city? Would anyone accept me as a friend or a colleague? Let alone as a husband or lover? Suddenly I wanted to creep right back inside my nice safe shell and stay there. At least as a beggar I had a reasonably steady source of income – meagre, yes, but steady.

Maybe Jesus was watching my reaction. I wouldn't know. But when I'd been going round this loop for quite a while, he interrupted my train of thought. In fact it would be more accurate to say he derailed it!

'Open your eyes,' he commanded, 'and throw your begging bowl away.'

That's what did it. The prospect of parting company with my begging bowl, my alter ego, my only friend. I opened my eyes, sure enough, but no light came in, just tears flowed out.

He caught me in his arms, and held me, while I sobbed out my fears.

'I don't think I could survive outside this little world I live in,' I confessed.

'I know,' he calmed me. 'I know, and I tell you, you can, if you want to.'

And that was the miracle. Not exactly what I had in mind, but I knew then that it was a now-or-never choice. I could stay blind, and relatively safe. Or I could have my sight, and all the risk and responsibility of a fuller human life. I felt the strength and the power of his arms holding me. This man was the real McCoy, a fully human being. I knew my choice was made. I wanted to be like him.

I nodded my head.

He placed my begging bowl in my hand and squeezed my arm.

I hurled the bowl away with all the strength I could muster.

I turned to him.

And his eyes were gazing into mine, full of love and power.

He had brown eyes.

I'll never forget him.

Margaret Silf
Roots and Wings:
The Human Journey from a Speck of Stardust to a Spark of God

**MONDAY
MARCH 3**

**FOURTH WEEK
OF LENT**

Isaiah 65: 17-21

*Psalm 30: 1-5,
10-12*

John 4: 43-54

Now there was a royal official whose son lay ill in Capernaum. When he heard that Jesus had come from Judea to Galilee, he went and begged him to come down and heal his son, for he was at the point of death…. The official said to him, "Sir, come down before my little boy dies." Jesus said to him, "Go; your son will live."

John 4: 46-47, 49-50

I'm encouraged by Henri Nouwen's words that we must trust our stories, believe that they deserve to be told and that the better we tell them the better we will want to live them. Merton said it was his vocation to remain a witness to the nobility of the private person, its primacy over the group. I disagree with those who say religion's a cop-out, a form of denial. While religion may be a refuge for some people afraid of going to hell, I cling to the old adage that spirituality is for people who have already been there. Each of us must create our own spiritual map. Rembrandt painted 63 self-portraits – not to save model fees, but to savour the spiritual within himself, plumb his own soul. In revisiting the same themes in these kaddishes, circling round the jagged rock of your suicide, little by little I'm learning to understand not so much the "why" but, as Nouwen put it, to "stand under" the grief, hold it without being in control. And more and more Blake's words that we were put on earth

"for a little space that we may learn to bear the beams of love" strikes a chord. We may never adequately understand or define love, but as Gerald May wrote, we are meant to live into life's meaning. Like Michelangelo's sculpture "The Awakening Storm," which shows a body struggling to emerge from stone, I want to break free from my prison of fear, find the sunlit uplands of wholeness and love. Trapeze artists are not afraid to let go, brave the emptiness of space, trust that someone will be there to catch them. By embracing my shadow side and befriending your death (and all our deaths) I'm slowly learning to face fear and take back my life. We can choose the terminal, snuff out life and spirit, or we can name our deaths, grieve them and let them give us back a blessing.

James Clarke
A Mourner's Kaddish: Suicide and the Rediscovery of Hope

TUESDAY MARCH 4

FOURTH WEEK OF LENT

Ezekiel 47: 1-9, 12

Psalm 46: 1-8

John 5: 1-16

Jesus said, "Do you want to be made well?" The sick man answered him, "Sir, I have no one to put me into the pool when the water is stirred up…." Jesus said, "Stand up, take your mat and walk." At once the man was made well, and he took up his mat and began to walk.

John 5: 6-9

Most of us do not experience our decision in such dramatic terms. We may begin to follow Christ half-heartedly at first, perhaps just obscuring him from a distance, hanging around at the edge of the crowd. We may try to postpone the final commitment as long as we can. But, in the end, this is what it always comes down to: a moment of irrevocable choice. The choice is presented to us from outside of ourselves: as a challenge, a grace that we have done nothing to deserve and even, perhaps, have not asked for. But the response is always ours to give, and it must always be given freely. The decision must come from us. The call to follow Christ is an invitation to love, and love, like trust, is always free. It must come from within: from the truth of our own being, our own heart.

Irma Zaleski
Finding Christ Within

Wednesday March 5

Fourth Week of Lent

Isaiah 49: 8-15

Psalm 145: 8-18

John 5: 16-30

> "Very truly, I tell you, the hour is coming, and is now here, when the dead will hear the voice of the Son of God, and those who hear will live."
>
> *John 5: 25*

Spirit of the deeps,
You call out to me to test Your infinity.
Mark your steps, You say.
Start out slowly,
because once started,
there is no end but joy.
It is like a woman in labour:
once the first step is taken,
there is no stopping it,
a long, slow drawing out
of the deep mysteries of life.

This is God's pedagogy of time:
time moving relentlessly,
time standing still in the midst of movement,
time vanishing as mystery takes hold,
time emptied even of longing.

Live in this infinity of time.
Let mystery meet mystery;
something deep within will respond.
And then, where else can I feel at home?
Spirit of the deeps, reach, touch, draw, hold.

(Inspired by Hadewijch of Brabant)

Mary T. Malone
Praying with the Women Mystics

**THURSDAY
MARCH 6**

**FOURTH WEEK
OF LENT**

Exodus 32: 7-14

Psalm 106: 19-23

John 5: 18, 31-47

The Jewish leaders were seeking to kill Jesus, because he was not only breaking the sabbath, but was also calling God his own Father, thereby making himself equal to God.

John 5: 18

Often, throughout this gospel, the phrase "the Jews" refers to people who do not believe in Jesus and are opposed to him. Such use of the phrase has had disastrous consequences for Christian–Jewish relations over the centuries, for it has contributed to Christian notions that "the Jews" are responsible for the death of Jesus, notions that are not true historically....

The author of the Gospel of John, however, who was likely a Jew, may be using this phrase simply as a way of identifying a group that is opposed to his or her group of Jews who do believe that Jesus is the Messiah. Thus, the intent of the phrase was not to promote anti-Semitism, but to distance the author's community from other groups that had different beliefs. In fact, many think that the Gospel of John was produced by a group of Jews who had been expelled from the synagogue because they accepted Jesus as the Messiah. This rejection by the synagogue may have led them to vilify those who had excluded them for their beliefs and to focus the gospel on the key contentious issue: the identity of Jesus.

Alicia Batten
Teachings of Jesus

**FRIDAY
MARCH 7**

Jesus cried out as he was teaching in the temple, "You know me, and you know where I am from. I have not come on my own. But the one who sent me is true, and you do not know him. I know him, because I am from him, and he sent me."

John 7: 28-29

**FOURTH WEEK
OF LENT**

*Wisdom 2: 1,
12-22*

Psalm 34: 16-22

*John 7: 1-2, 10,
25-30*

Christ did not come to replace the God of the Hebrews or nullify the need for any further search for God. He did not hand to us the whole solution to the mystery of God. He only pointed to himself and said, "I am the Way." In other words, Christ came to show us in his own person, in his own words and his own life and death, how we can find God who is beyond all concepts or images, beyond all human definitions or beliefs: who is unimaginable.

This is a fundamental principle of our faith that we must never forget. We search for Christ, we long to find him, we enter into a relationship with him not because he is the greatest, the most wonderful, the most kind and loving – and whatever other virtue we may think of – human being who has ever lived. We search for Christ and struggle to know and love him because, and only because, in him we encounter and recognize God. Christ is the Truth at the heart of all reality.

Irma Zaleski
Finding Christ Within

Saturday March 8

Fourth Week of Lent

Jeremiah 11: 18-20

Psalm 7: 1-2, 8-11

John 7: 40-53

The temple police went back to the chief priests and Pharisees, who asked them, "Why did you not arrest him?" The police answered, "Never has anyone spoken like this!"

John 7: 45-46

Two Greek words are used to distinguish between these two expressions of power. *Exousia* is externally sanctioned, hierarchical "power over"; *dunamis* is inner "power with," the result of deep inner strength that transforms fear into agapic love. "Understanding nonviolent power is being awake to the difference between *dunamis* and *exousia*," [Leonard] Desroches says. He adds that *dunamis* is "the inner God-given power that we are all created with – dignity; and *exousia* [is] socially sanctioned power, public authority which may or may not be good, depending on the extent to which is it used as radical service."

Desroches is a perfect example of a modern-day prophet of nonviolence. He has used his prophetic call-response, this gift and this grace, in conjunction with his talents of speaking and writing about nonviolence, to touch many people. In his ongoing deepening of his spirituality of nonviolence, he sees nonviolence as the real force in Jesus' Third Way.

Janet Malone
Transforming Conflict and Anger into Peace and Nonviolence: A Spiritual Direction

SUNDAY MARCH 9

FIFTH SUNDAY OF LENT

Ezekiel 37: 12-14

Psalm 130: 1-8

Romans 8: 8-11

John 11: 1-45

When Martha heard that Jesus was coming, she went and met him and said, "Lord, if you had been here, my brother would not have died. But even now I know that God will give you whatever you ask of him." Jesus said to her, "Your brother will rise again."

John 11: 20-23

When Jesus goes to Bethany to Lazarus' home, Martha and then Mary meet him. Both upbraid him for not using his powers to save their brother from death. But Jesus' call is not to manifest his powers, but to live out his relationship with his Father. Jesus can raise Lazarus from the dead, as he raised two others. But like those two others, Lazarus would eventually die again. Jesus' relationship with the Father allows for resurrection. That relationship manifests a love so strong that death cannot overcome it. One enters into death journeying towards a love beyond name and imagining, and that love enters into death to bring the beloved into that new creation called resurrection. That new creation is not the cyclical return of natural rhythms, nor is it the miraculous raising up of the dead back into earthly life. It is something new, and it attests to the transforming creativity of the Father. In the Lazarus story Jesus manifests that greater gift the Father has for us. It is a gift that does not ignore the wretchedness of a disordered world or the ravages of sin and death and their effects on all of us. Instead, it enters into those places of crisis and takes away their power, making them doorways – however painful and powerful – into new life.

The risk the Father takes with Mary and Martha in denying them immediate access to Jesus' power is the risk the Father takes with each of us. If we are indulged with instant gratification because we know God loves us, and we love God, we reduce God to being a magician and ourselves to a narcissism that ignores the world's suffering. This approach overlooks God's mysterious will to enter into that suffering as a human being, and to endure it even to a humiliating and painful death on a cross. It does not admit that we are invited to follow Christ in living out his passion for the Father, or that intimacy with Christ makes us more human, not less – more aware of the destructiveness of evil but also more aware of the depths of God's love.

John Pungente SJ and Monty Williams SJ
Finding God in the Dark:
Taking the Spiritual Exercises of St. Ignatius to the Movies

**MONDAY
MARCH 10**

FIFTH WEEK
OF LENT

Daniel 13

Psalm 23: 1-6

John 8: 1-11

Jesus said, "Woman, where are they? Has no one condemned you?" She said, "No one, sir." Jesus said, "Neither do I condemn you. Go your way, and from now on do not sin again."
John 8: 10-11

Jesus begins with a humble question
in order to enter into relationship with her....
Then Jesus affirms that he does not condemn
her either.

Does that mean that Jesus does not see
adultery as wrong?
No, what Jesus wants is to liberate people
so that they change their ways
and discover their real value as human
beings and as children of God.
Jesus does not want this woman
to grovel in guilt,
but to admit that she has done something wrong,
and to discover that she is forgiven,
that she can be free of guilt.
Then she can go free knowing
she is a precious person
called to love God, her husband,
her children and her neighbours,
and to give life to others.
Changed, she can stand up and be herself,
for she has discovered that Jesus loves her.

Jean Vanier
*Drawn into the Mystery of Jesus
through the Gospel of John*

TUESDAY MARCH 11

FIFTH WEEK OF LENT

Numbers 21: 4-9

Psalm 102: 1-2, 15-20

John 8: 21-30

Jesus said to them, "You are from below, I am from above; you are of this world, I am not of this world. I told you that you would die in your sins, for you will die in your sins unless you believe that I am he."

They said to him, "Who are you?"
John 8: 23-25

In my own mind, and my own heart, there is actually no doubt that Jesus of Nazareth, the human person who lived fully true to what it means to be human, moved beyond death to become the Christ, a presence who now transcends time and space, and is in the eternal now, for ever at one with the source and destiny of life. How this happened, in physical and metaphysical terms, is Mystery, and I am prepared to allow it to be so, knowing that my mind is far too under-evolved to fathom its depths.

However, we do know, from twenty-first-century physics, that energy and matter are interchangeable, and that all that is may manifest itself in forms of particles or waves – particles of 'matter' (for example the particles that form a human person who can be identified and related to) or waves of energy with no permanent physical position. I find no difficulty in believing that Jesus of Nazareth consciously reached this point of transcendence, and continues to be present to receptive hearts and minds, always drawing us, too, towards our own transcendence.

In the mystery of resurrection, Jesus transcends the historic person, the unique configuration of particles, and becomes a wave of pure energy – the energy of Love itself – the energy that many call the Holy Spirit. The historic person of Jesus becomes the Christ, the anointed one, the one who is completely at one with the source of all being, and calls all who have ears to hear and hearts to respond, to grow in and through that Spirit into the same fullness of life.

Margaret Silf
Roots and Wings:
The Human Journey from a Speck of Stardust to a Spark of God

Wednesday March 12

FIFTH WEEK OF LENT

Daniel 3: 13-20, 24, 49-56, 91-95

Daniel 3: 52-56

John 8: 31-42

Jesus said, "Very truly, I tell you, everyone who commits sin is a slave to sin. The slave does not have a permanent place in the household; the son has a place there forever. So if the Son makes you free, you will be free indeed."

John 8: 34-36

Like most contemporary Christians, I found it difficult to feel comfortable with the notion of being a sinner. I was aware, of course, that I had often committed wrong, perhaps even evil, acts: I have broken the commandments and needed to repent and make amends. I had often failed at being kind or loving or forgiving enough. I was not always faithful in fulfilling my duties; I did not always tell the truth. Yet the notion of being a sinner all the time – being defined as a sinner and having to repent for it – did not seem reasonable to me. Rather, it seemed to be an expression of a very gloomy and judgmental view of human nature that I had never found convincing or appealing.

But now I realized that praying so constantly, so insistently, for mercy, I was repenting for more than any specific sins I may have committed. I was not accusing myself of being evil – of being "stuffed with evil" – but acknowledging that I, like all human beings, was tainted with it. I too had turned away – had become alienated – from God and from my own reality again and again.

→

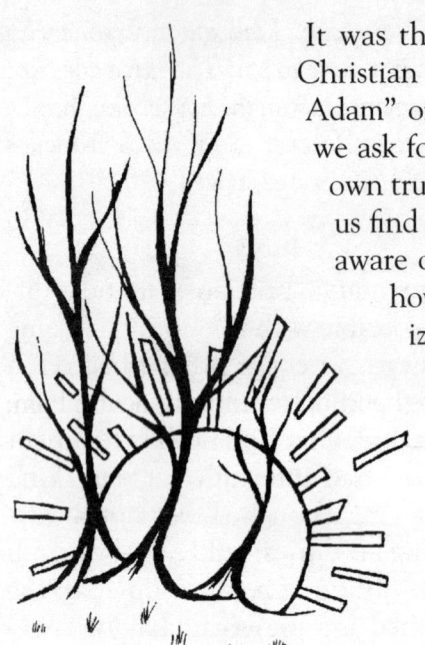

It was this state of alienation that early Christian teachers referred to as "the sin of Adam" or "the human condition." When we ask for mercy, we are not rejecting our own true reality but asking Christ to help us find it. We are asking him to make us aware of all our alienation and teach us how to let go of it. And so, we realize, we have discovered the ancient Christian path of conversion: the path of becoming truly real by facing our unreality and stripping ourselves of it – repenting of it – bit by bit.

Irma Zaleski
Finding Christ Within

THURSDAY MARCH 13

FIFTH WEEK OF LENT

Genesis 17: 3-9

Psalm 105: 4-9

John 8: 51-59

Then the Jews said to him, "You are not yet fifty years old, and have you seen Abraham?" Jesus said to them, "Very truly, I tell you, before Abraham was, I am."

John 8: 57-58

Each of us has a core set of beliefs about who and what and why we are…. I have thought long and hard about these realities of self, and finally was able to write my own set of "I ams": I am stardust flowing out of the heart of divinity. I am who I am; it is by being who I am that I discover my authentic identity. I am called into intimacy, energetic love, and an ever-deepening capacity to embrace and celebrate my as-yet-unlived life. I am called out of the fetal waters of fear, doubt, repression and hesitation to be reborn as a new me, a new relationship, a new life, a new plant, a new "I am." I am invited to live in a world that is inclusive, a place of belonging that empowers me and others, that celebrates accomplishments, that is fuelled by hope, and that is identified by the touchstone categories of reciprocity and mutual enhancement. I am summoned to participate in the reinvention of humanity, to confront this withering moment in history with freedom and courage and an ever-deepening capacity to bring forth a world that is not yet but will become.

James Conlon
*From the Stars to the Street:
Engaged Wisdom for a Brokenhearted World*

FRIDAY MARCH 14

FIFTH WEEK OF LENT

Jeremiah 20: 7, 10-13

Psalm 18: 1-6

John 10: 31-42

The Jews took up stones again to stone him. Jesus replied, "I have shown you many good works from the Father. For which of these are you going to stone me?" The Jews answered, "It is not for a good work that we are going to stone you, but for blasphemy, because you, though only a human being, are making yourself God."

John 10: 31-33

Some Sundays
I go looking for God
on the new quays
in old Wexford.

I always have Marguerite in mind.
Look at the Seine, she said;
it rises and takes its travels
through field, town, forest,
and finally reaches Paris
on its way to the sea.
All the time it is called the Seine.
That is its name.

Then the miracle happens:
the Seine reaches the sea
and the Seine loses its own name.
It becomes nameless,
as it mingles
water with water in the vast moving sea.
And no one can tell
where the river ends and the sea begins.
And so it is with me, she mused.

I have my own name,
my journey through life,
my travels,
and then, in my seeking,
like the river,
I enter the vast moving sea of God
and no one can tell
where I end and God begins.

There I am, God and I,
my nameless self lost
in the vast sea of God's presence.
and who can tell, then,
where God ends and I begin?

And so, on some Sundays,
I look at the Slaney,
following its own course
from Lugnaquilla to the sea,
through Wicklow hills and Carlow towns,
and Wexford farms,
past Enniscorthy Castle and cathedrals
and so on to Wexford,
where its waters mingle with the sea,
and then it is Slaney no more.

And there, standing on the quay,
I try to see myself, as Marguerite did,
lost and unnamed and mingled in God,
freely swimming in a sea of divinity,
not knowing nor needing to know
where humanity ends and God begins,
where I end and God begins.

Sometimes, then, I turn townward
with my back to the Slaney-sea
and gaze the length of the quays,
from Crescent Pool,
past mussel boats,
to the graceful low-slung bridge.
And there,
right in the middle of the quays,
I try to imagine a woman
being burned to death
on the Wexford quays,
just as Marguerite was –
right there in the middle of the Place de Grève
in her beloved Paris,
on the first day of June
in the year 1310.

How to imagine such a horror.
How to imagine the fear that one lone woman
could evoke in the fierce, fiery, fear-filled church.

Was it because she spoke of swimming in divinity?
Was it because her chosen name for her God
was Lady-Love?
Was it because, as a woman,
she dared to teach about her Woman-God of Love?

How could they have been so terrified
of this one woman, Marguerite,
whose calm acceptance of her horrific death
silenced the onlookers into awed reverence?

That day, the Seine provided no answers,
and today, turning again towards the sea-bound Slaney,
I seek, not answers,
but some small share of her God-lost self,
some sense of her all-embracing briny divinity,
some feeling that here,
in Wexford, between Slaney and sea
I will learn to keep looking
and not miss the great moment of mingling.

(Inspired by Marguerite Porete)

Mary T. Malone
Praying with the Women Mystics

Saturday March 15

Fifth Week of Lent

2 Samuel 7: 4-5, 12-16

Psalm 89: 1-4, 26-28

Romans 4: 13, 16-18, 22

Matthew 1: 16-21, 24

An angel of the Lord appeared to him in a dream and said, "Joseph, son of David, do not be afraid to take Mary as your wife, for the child conceived in her is from the Holy Spirit. She will bear a son, and you are to name him Jesus, for he will save his people from their sins."

When Joseph awoke from sleep, he did as the angel of the Lord commanded him.
                            Matthew 1: 20-21, 24

You know what is within us, O God.
You know the beauty
and the falseness
of our hearts.
You know the
heights and depths
of the human spirit.
Lead us further
into the universe
of our souls
that we may
know the wisdom
and strength
that you have placed within us.
Lead us further into the mystery of our souls
that we may be strong and wise
for the well-being of the world.

J. Philip Newell
Celtic Treasure

Sunday March 16

Passion Sunday

When they had come near Jerusalem, Jesus sent two disciples, saying, "Go into the village ahead of you, and immediately you will find a donkey tied, and a colt with her; untie them and bring them to me…."

This took place to fulfill what had been spoken through the prophet, saying, "Tell the daughter of Zion, Look, your king is coming to you, humble, and mounted on a donkey, and on a colt, the foal of a donkey."

Matthew 21: 1-2, 4-5

Matthew 21: 1-11

Isaiah 50: 4-7

Psalm 22: 7-8, 16-23

Philippians 2: 6-11

Matthew 26: 14 – 27: 66

When Jesus performed the miracle
of the multiplication of bread and fish,
the crowd wanted to make him king,
but he fled from them.
Jesus did not come to exercise a temporal
and social power.
He came to reveal the truth of the God of love
and the Love of God.
It is only when he is bound in ropes,
that he accepts the title of king.
He is an imprisoned king, a vulnerable king,
a king with no earthly power.
He is the king of love
who wants to communicate his love
in and through his weakness and vulnerability.
He is a king yearning
for the communion of hearts.

This is the truth he has come to proclaim.
Not power for the sake of power,
but to build a world of love at the service
of the communion of hearts,
the power of love
and compassion that heals,
liberates and gives life,
that calls people to live
in love with him.

We are all called to live
a deep friendship
with this vulnerable king.
That is why
Jesus came to be with us.
Yet so often we want to be on the winning side
and would like to have a triumphant king,
a triumphant Christianity,
a triumphant church that imposes laws and has global influence.
Like Peter we can be ashamed of our humiliated king.
And like him we can learn from our humiliation.
Perhaps it is only those who are humiliated and excluded
who see in the humiliated king their friend and saviour.

Jean Vanier
Drawn into the Mystery of Jesus through the Gospel of John

MONDAY MARCH 17

HOLY WEEK

Isaiah 42: 1-7

Psalm 27: 1-3, 13-15

John 12: 1-11

> *Mary took a pound of costly perfume made of pure nard, anointed Jesus' feet, and wiped them with her hair. The house was filled with the fragrance of the perfume. But Judas Iscariot, one of his disciples (the one who was about to betray him), said, "Why was this perfume not sold for three hundred denarii and the money given to the poor?"*
>
> John 12: 3-5

Despite doubts and intimations to the contrary, I cling to the belief in the essential goodness of life that nothing, no matter how horrendous, can destroy. Though we have limited control over the circumstances of our lives, I believe we still retain the power to shape our attitude towards what befalls us, affirm life no matter what happens. So the central question for me becomes not the meaning of your suicide, but the meaning of my life. Despair, stoic resignation, compulsive distraction are not the only choices. As Victor Frankl put it, "Man doesn't merely exist, but always decides what his existence will be, what he will become in the next moment." Though I can't accept that God willed your suicide or suffering (or anyone else's, for that matter), I still believe in the human capacity to respond in ways that bear witness to the core reality of creation – love.

Though it is not always self-evident, I like to think that your suicide shook us out of our anomie, uncovered portions of humanity in us that had lain dormant and in some ways made us stronger, more caring people. Paradoxically, you could say your death quickened us to life. I say yes, yes to life now and everlasting. In the end it all comes back to "letting go" and trusting, as Julian of Norwich put it, that "all shall be well and all shall be well and all manner of things shall be well."

James Clarke
*A Mourner's Kaddish:
Suicide and the
Rediscovery of Hope*

**TUESDAY
MARCH 18**

HOLY WEEK

Isaiah 49: 1-6

*Psalm 71: 1-5,
15-17*

*John 13: 21-33,
36-38*

Jesus said, "Where I am going, you cannot follow me now; but you will follow afterward." Peter said to him, "Lord, why can I not follow you now? I will lay down my life for you."

Jesus answered, "Very truly, before the cock crows, you will have denied me three times."
John 13: 36-38

If we are to be disciples of Christ, then we must do what our Teacher has called us to do; we must follow his teaching as well as we can. But each one of us must embrace and follow it in the way that is true to us: that expresses our own deepest truth.

And here, I believe, lies the greatest challenge of our spiritual lives: we do not really know how to be true to ourselves.... We do not know how to love and trust ourselves in the simple, uncomplicated way that small children accept themselves.... We need to remind ourselves that being imperfect and weak does not disqualify us from being beloved in the eyes of Christ.

We need to learn that our far-from-perfect self, which we have such difficulty loving and accepting, has been created by God to play a part – perhaps a very small and yet an essential part – in incarnating a little bit of Christ in the world. We must, therefore, accept *all* of ourselves – the perfect and the imperfect – with respect and gratitude.

Irma Zaleski
Finding Christ Within

WEDNESDAY MARCH 19

HOLY WEEK

Isaiah 50: 4-9

Psalm 69: 7-9, 20-21, 30-33

Matthew 26: 14-26

One of the twelve, who was called Judas Iscariot, went to the chief priests and said, "What will you give me if I betray him to you?" They paid him thirty pieces of silver.

Matthew 26: 14-15

Nobody is totally good or totally bad. Judas, like all human beings, had his weak points. It is clear and affirmed in all four gospels that Judas betrayed Jesus. It is obviously a very sad thing to betray the person who had called him and shown him full confidence. To betray a person is seen in all cultures as something repulsive. But how Judas came to this point is far from clear. Some of the texts insist that he was too attached to money, and even that he was a thief. They thus suggest that this motive may have led him to betray Jesus. Human history is full of such cases: people are capable of doing terrible things just for the money.... But we still may wonder if Judas' love of money was truly what led him to betray Jesus. When he agreed to follow Jesus, he must have given up his job, whatever that was. He must have known that there was not much chance for him to become rich by following Jesus. That suggests that he was detached from money, but it does not necessarily rule out his becoming greedy later.

But not all texts suggest that money was the reason for his betrayal of Jesus. We can then only guess at what may have been the deep reason for such a change in the life of Judas, from disciple to traitor. All leaders have a support group: political leaders and also spiritual leaders, such as the prophets. Jesus had his support group, and Judas was part of it. But members of such support groups may leave their leader for all kinds of reasons, especially out of disappointment with the leader. It may be that Judas became disappointed in Jesus: in his person, in his ministry, in his preaching, in his behaviour, or some other dimension. This of course does not justify Judas' betrayal of Jesus as leader. Judas could have opted simply to quit the group.

Walter Vogels
Biblical Human Failures: Lot, Samson, Saul, Jonah, Judas

THURSDAY MARCH 20

HOLY THURSDAY

Exodus 12: 1-8, 11-14

Psalm 116: 12-18

1 Corinthians 11: 23-26

John 13: 1-15

Beloved: I received from the Lord what I also handed on to you, that the Lord Jesus on the night when he was betrayed took a loaf of bread, and when he had given thanks, he broke it and said, "This is my body that is for you. Do this in remembrance of me."

In the same way he took the cup also, after supper, saying, "This cup is the new covenant in my blood. Do this, as often as you drink it, in remembrance of me." For as often as you eat this bread and drink the cup, you proclaim the Lord's death until he comes.

1 Corinthians 11: 23-26

What Jesus does at the Passover meal is what every one of us does at our family celebrations. We remember the past with the ones who share life with us, and each year we bring something new to that gathering. We bring what has happened to each of us, and we tend to discuss those happenings in that ritual context so that they become part of that occasion.

The ritual gathering on that particular evening becomes more than the celebration of surviving another year under Roman occupation, more than the revival of the hope of yet another liberation from foreign oppression. For Christ, it allows the entry into a new dispensation that allows us freedom in the world, but not the freedom of worldly standards and methods. With the meal he offers, he gives the way of being united with God in more than just memory and ritual. In making the bread and wine he blesses real manifestations of himself, he ensures that his essence remains with those with whom he shares his life and mission. We become what we eat. And what we become is partakers of the same relationship that he has with the Father. It gives a peace the world cannot give, and a rootedness that transcends this world's limitations.

In that rootedness lies freedom and focus. When we love someone, we open ourselves to that person. We give our very selves over to the beloved. We become the beloved, and the beloved, in accepting our gift, becomes us. In Jesus' founding of this new ritual using the elements of the Passover meal, our unity with God is established in a way that is as real and as physical as our own bodies.

**John Pungente SJ
and Monty Williams SJ**
*Finding God in the Dark:
Taking the Spiritual Exercises
of St. Ignatius to the Movies*

**FRIDAY
MARCH 21**

GOOD FRIDAY

Isaiah
52: 13 – 53: 12

Psalm 31: 1, 5,
11-16, 24

Hebrews 4: 14-16;
5: 7-9

John
18: 1 – 19: 42

After this, in order to fulfill the scripture, Jesus said, "I am thirsty." So they put a sponge full of [sour] wine on a branch of hyssop and held it to his mouth. When Jesus had received the wine, he said, "It is finished."

John 19: 28-30

Right at the beginning of John's Gospel, Jesus met the Samaritan woman at the well and he said to her, 'Give me water.' At the beginning and the end of the story Jesus asks us to satisfy his thirst. This is how God comes to us, in a thirsty person wanting something that we have to give. God's relationship with creation is entirely that of gift. To be in friendship with us, and friendship always implies equality. And so the one who gives us everything invites us into friendship by asking for a gift back, whatever we may have to give.... There is an African proverb that the hand that gives is always uppermost and the hand that receives is lower down. God makes friendship with us by coming to us as one who begs for what we have.

Most of all he wants us. Usually we think that reaching God is hard work. We must earn forgiveness; we must become good, otherwise he will disapprove of us. But this is wrong. God comes to us before we have ever turned to him. God thirsts for our love. He is racked with desire for us.

Timothy Radcliffe
Seven Last Words

SATURDAY MARCH 22

HOLY SATURDAY

Ezekiel 36: 16-28

Psalm 42: 4;
43: 3-4

Romans 6: 3-11

Matthew 28: 1-10

> *We know that our old self was crucified with him so that the body of sin might be destroyed, and we might no longer be enslaved to sin. For whoever has died is freed from sin. But if we have died with Christ, we believe that we will also live with him.*
>
> Romans 6: 6-8

Christ did not abolish death; he did not take it away from us, for death is the natural end of all finite life. Neither did he take away from us the fear of death that we share with every living creature.

Christ faced this same fear as he lay sweating blood in the Garden, and he had to face it alone, as we all will have to face it one day.... Only Christ can share our fear and our death with us and conquer it in us as he conquered it in himself. By suffering death in its full horror, Christ filled it with his own victory and thus removed its sting. Death, he showed us, however painful and terrifying it may be, is not the end, and we are not alone. Christ abides within our death as fully as he abides within our life and gives it its true meaning. When, shining with the light and glory of heaven, Christ rose from the tomb, he blessed our death and changed it forever. He consecrated it, making it into a meeting place of time and eternity: a mystery-event.

Irma Zaleski
Finding Christ Within

SUNDAY MARCH 23

EASTER SUNDAY

Acts 10: 34-43

Psalm 118: 1-2, 16-17, 22-23

Colossians 3: 1-4

1 Corinthians 5: 6-8

John 20: 1-18

Mary Magdalene stood weeping outside the tomb.... Jesus said to her, "Mary!" She turned and said to him in Hebrew, "Rabbouni!" which means Teacher.

John 20: 11, 16

According to Eckhart, Mary, seeking God, stood at the tomb weeping, looking for something she could not find. The one she sought she did not find. The corpse was gone, and instead of the body that she sought, there were two living angels. This ineffable experience of loss is what the soul desires to name but is unable to name....

When we know the divine nearness, our former pleasures no longer satisfy us and we long to be freed from whatever holds us back. As St. Augustine says, "Our hears are restless until they rest in you, O Lord" (*Confessions* Bk. VI). We desire God alone. Nothing else will do. No passing things will do. Nothing but the light of divine presence will do. When we want God, everything else becomes less desirable. The things we might have desired before we were aware of God's presence in our life now no longer seem desirable.... We find it difficult to see how we could so desire God that everything else is turned completely around, especially what normally gives us pleasure. This is a key aspect of the will, or the soul's desire for God. It is the paradox of the gospel.

Michael Demkovich OP
Introducing Meister Eckhart

REFERENCES

Angus, Charlie. *Les Costello: Canada's Flying Father*. Ottawa: Novalis, 2005. (February 27)

Batten, Alicia. *Teachings of Jesus*. Ottawa: Novalis, 2005. (March 6)

Chittister, Joan D. *In the Heart of the Temple*. Grand Rapids, MI/Ottawa: Wm. B. Eerdmans/Novalis, 2004. (February 24)

Chittister, Joan D. *Scarred by Struggle, Transformed by Hope*. Grand Rapids, MI/Ottawa: Wm. B. Eerdmans/Novalis, 2003. (February 13)

Clarke, Bill, SJ. *Enough Room for Joy: The Early Days of L'Arche*. Ottawa: Novalis, 2006. (February 20)

Clarke, James. *A Mourner's Kaddish: Suicide and the Rediscovery of Hope*. Ottawa: Novalis, 2006. (March 3, 17)

Cocks, Nancy. *Invisible We See You: Tracing Celtic Threads Through Christian Community*. Ottawa: Novalis, 2006. (February 25)

Conlon, James. *From the Stars to the Street: Engaged Wisdom for a Brokenhearted World*. Ottawa: Novalis, 2007. (March 13)

Dear, John, SJ. "Henri the Peacemaker," in *Remembering Henri: The Life and Legacy of Henri Nouwen*. Gerald S. Twomey and Claude Pomerleau (eds.), Maryknoll, NY/Ottawa: Orbis/Novalis, 2006. (February 6, 28)

Demkovich, Michael, OP. *Introducing Meister Eckhart*. Ottawa: Novalis, 2005. (February 29, March 23)

de Waal, Esther. *Lost in Wonder*. Norwich, UK/Ottawa: Canterbury Press/Novalis, 2003. (February 23)

Malone, Janet. *Transforming Conflict and Anger into Peace and Nonviolence: A Spiritual Direction*. Ottawa: Novalis, 2007. (February 15, 18, March 8)

Malone, Mary T. *Praying with the Women Mystics*. Blackrock, Ireland/Ottawa: Columba/Novalis, 2006. (February 19, March 5, 14)

McLaughlin, John L. *Parables of Jesus*. Ottawa: Novalis, 2004. (March 1)

McRae-McMahon, Dorothy. *Celebrations Along the Way: Liturgies for Everyday Moments*. Ottawa: Novalis, 2001. (February 9)

Newell, J. Philip. *Celtic Treasure*. Norwich, UK/Ottawa: Canterbury Press/Novalis, 2005. (March 15)

Parker, Shane. *Answering the Big Questions*. Ottawa: Novalis, 2005. (Introduction, February 12)

Pungente, John, SJ, and Monty Williams, SJ. *Finding God in the Dark: Taking the Spiritual Exercises of St. Ignatius to the Movies*. Ottawa: Novalis, 2004. (February 10, March 9, 20)

Radcliffe, Timothy, OP. *Seven Last Words*. Ottawa: Novalis, 2004. (February 26, March 21)

Silf, Margaret. *Roots and Wings: The Human Journey from a Speck of Stardust to a Spark of God*. London/Ottawa: Darton, Longman and Todd/Novalis, 2006. (February 11, 14, 21, March 2, 11)

Vanier, Jean. *Befriending the Stranger*. Ottawa: Novalis, 2005. (February 7)

_____. *Drawn into the Mystery of Jesus through the Gospel of John*. Ottawa: Novalis, 2004. (March 10, 16)

Vogels, Walter. *Biblical Human Failures: Lot, Samson, Saul, Jonah, Judas*. Ottawa: Novalis, 2007. (March 19)

Williams, Rowan. *The Dwelling of the Light: Praying with Icons of Christ*. Norwich, UK/Ottawa: Canterbury Press/Novalis, 2003. (February 17)

Zaleski, Irma. *Finding Christ Within*. Ottawa: Novalis, 2007. (February 8, 16, 22, March 4, 7, 12, 18, 22)

ORDERING INFORMATION

In Canada, you may order any of the titles listed in this booklet from:

> Novalis
> 10 Lower Spadina Avenue
> Suite 400
> Toronto, ON M5V 2Z2

Toll free
   Tel: 1-800-387-7164   •   Fax: 1-800-204-4140

E-mail
   books@novalis.ca

Website
   www.novalis.ca

NOTE

When ordering from outside Canada, please contact us for the distributor in your own country.

Living with Christ

SACRED JOURNEY
A NOVALIS TREASURY

Sacred Journey is a mini-anthology that includes reflections, prayers, short essays and brief excerpts drawn from longer works. Designed for daily use, this Novalis treasury includes the details of each day's scripture readings along with a related reflection by a celebrated Novalis author. This Lent, let *Sacred Journey* guide your reflection as you travel the road to Jerusalem, and to the celebration of new life!

€ 2·00

ISBN 978-2-89507-912-5

Lent 2008